Contents

Introduction..................................4

Basics...5

Tools and materials.........................7

Crystals 9

Twinkling, light, and airy 10
Crimp your style with sparkling possibilities

Diamonds and pearls............................13
Pair crystals and pearls for twice the dazzling elegance

Channel the brilliance of crystals 14
Link crystal and channel-set components to make a vivid necklace and earrings

Clear winner 17
Favorite colors meet in a sparkling design

For a special day....................................20
An intricate choker is perfect for a formal occasion

Monet's colors bloom in a
crystal necklace....................................23
WireLace provides a flexible landscape for a pastel palette

Focus on simple elegance 26
A dramatic crystal filigree component anchors softly draped chains

Diamond alternative 30
Chunky crystals are almost better than the real thing

Light and lively....................................31
Make a lightweight silver-and-crystal necklace with matching earrings

Extended style 34
One long strand glimmers without end

Pearls 37

Knot this time 38
Try your hand at something new

Pretty in pink and plum........................41
Play up the beauty of a single blossom in a fresh necklace and earrings

Pearls extend your style options 44
One superlong necklace offers multiple looks

Pearl solitaire....................................44
A single pearl gives luminescent simplicity

Pastel pearls....................................48
A pastel-hued necklace and earrings are a classic set

Subtle & classic 50
A variety of colors brightens up a chain-and-pearl jewelry set

Small touches add charm.....................54
Petal bead caps give a floral effect to a classic look

Pearls and chain 55
An asymetrical necklace takes pearls out of the classic realm

Pearls, interrupted....................................58
Searching through cast-off jewelry yields unexpected results

Pearls' night out 60
Dress up with a pearl choker and earrings

Wire 63

Sculpt a leaf necklace and earrings 64
Shape and assemble lengths of wire to create this necklace and earrings

Branch dressing....................................67
Craft a delicate collar of branches flecked with tiny gemstones

Tiers of joy 70
Teardrop components frame simple earrings

Maid to order....................................72
Customize earrings for a wedding party

Suspended briolette............................75
Dangle a drop of color in the center of a gracefully arching wire pendant

Briolettes unwrapped 78
A simple design turns top-drilled beads into earrings

Contributors 79

Introduction

Special occasions are often the high points of our lives, times when we celebrate, we see loved ones — and we dress up. So what better way to make your special occasion more memorable than to personalize it? Create your own beautiful jewelry for your next event, and you'll know that you crafted the perfect complement to your elegant ensemble.

The projects in *Making Elegant Jewelry for Special Occasions* are suited to proms and other dances, graduations, anniversary celebrations, quinceñaras, and formal parties. They're also ideal for weddings, whether you, yourself, are engaged, or if you're in a bridal party, the mother of the bride, or just know someone who is getting married. Anyone who's been to a bridal show knows that jewelry is a big part of the big day! Consider holding a beading party so the ladies of your bridal party can each make their own piece of jewelry for the ceremony. In fact, these pieces would be great to create with a group of friends at a beading party, no matter the occasion.

The jewelry designs featured in this book use some of the most popular materials available today, including crystals, pearls, and wire. That makes them adaptable — change up the colors of the crystals you choose to make earrings like Jill Alexander's "Briolettes unwrapped" work with any outfit. Simple crystal and chain designs like Arleen Bejerano's "Focus on simple elegance" will go as well with a casual sundress as they will with a gown. And with pieces like Naomi Fujimoto's "Pearls extend your style options," you can adjust the length and style of your necklace to fit whatever you're wearing. Versatile jewelry is a perfect staple for your own collection, and a great choice to create as gifts for friends and family!

There are plenty of options ahead, so turn the page and start creating your own elegant jewelry to make the next occasion in your life even more special!

Making Elegant Jewelry
for Special Occasions

pearls

crystals

wire

From the publisher
of *BeadStyle* magazine

KALMBACH BOOKS

Kalmbach Books
21027 Crossroads Circle
Waukesha, Wisconsin 53186
www.Kalmbach.com/Books

Published in 2010
14 13 12 11 10   1 2 3 4 5

Manufactured in the United States
of America

ISBN: 978-0-87116-425-4

Publisher's Cataloging-in-Publication Data

Making elegant jewelry for special occasions:
pearls, crystals, wire / from the publisher of
Beadstyle magazine.

   p. : ill. ; cm.

   ISBN: 978-0-87116-425-4

   1. Jewelry making--Handbooks, manuals,
etc. 2. Wire jewelry--Handbooks, manuals,
etc. 3. Wire jewelry--Patterns. 4. Beadwork--
Handbooks, manuals, etc. 5. Beadwork--
Patterns. 6. Pearls--Handbooks, manuals, etc..
I. Title: BeadStyle magazine.

TT212 .M35 2010
739.27

Basics

Cutting flexible beading wire

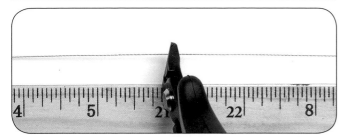

Decide how long you want your necklace to be. Add 6 in. (15cm) and cut a piece of beading wire to that length. (For a bracelet, add 5 in./13cm.)

Flattened crimp

1 Hold the crimp bead with the tip of your chainnose pliers. Squeeze the pliers firmly to flatten the crimp bead. Tug the clasp to make sure the

crimp has a solid grip on the wire. If the wire slides, remove the crimp bead and repeat with a new crimp bead.
2 The flattened crimp.

Folded crimp

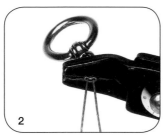

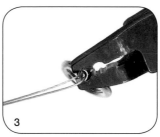

1 Position the crimp bead in the notch closest to the crimping pliers' handle.

2 Separate the wires and firmly squeeze the crimp bead.

3 Move the crimp bead into the notch at the pliers' tip. Squeeze the pliers, folding the bead in half at the indentation.

4 The folded crimp.

Opening a jump ring or loop

1 Hold the jump ring or loop with chainnose and round-nose pliers or two pairs of chainnose pliers.

2 To open the jump ring or loop, bring one pair of pliers toward you. Reverse the steps to close.

Surgeon's knot

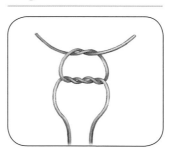

Cross the right end over the left and go through the loop. Go through again. Cross the left end over the right and go through. Pull the ends to tighten the knot.

Overhand knot

Make a loop and pass the working end through it. Pull the ends to tighten the knot.

Plain loop

1 Trim the wire ⅜ in. (1cm) above the top bead. Make a right-angle bend close to the bead.

2 Grab the wire's tip with roundnose pliers. Roll the wire to form a half circle.

3 Reposition the pliers in the loop and continue rolling, forming a centered circle above the bead.

4 The finished loop.

Wrapped loop

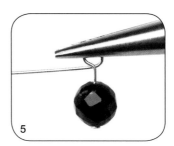 

1 Make sure there is at least 1¼ in. (3.2cm) of wire above the bead. With the tip of your chainnose pliers, grasp the wire directly above the bead. Bend the wire (above the pliers) into a right angle.

2 Position the jaws of your roundnose pliers vertically in the bend.

3 Bring the wire over the pliers' top jaw.

4 Reposition the pliers' lower jaw snugly in the curved wire. Wrap the wire down and around the bottom of the pliers. This is *the first half of a wrapped loop.*

5 Grasp the loop with chainnose pliers.

6 Wrap the wire tail around the wire stem, covering the stem between the loop and the top bead. Trim the excess wrapping wire, and press the end close to the stem with chainnose or crimping pliers.

Making a set of wraps above a top-drilled bead

1 Center a top-drilled bead on a 3-in. (7.6 cm) piece of wire. Bend each end upward, crossing the wires into an X.

2 Using chainnose pliers, make a small bend in each wire to form a right angle.

3 Wrap the horizontal wire around the vertical wire as in a wrapped loop. Trim the excess wrapping wire.

Tools and materials

The tools and materials you'll need for these projects are available in bead and craft stores, through catalogs, and online.

Tools

Chainnose pliers have smooth, flat inner jaws and tips that taper to a point so you can get into tiny spaces. Use them for gripping and for opening and closing loops and jump rings.

Crimping pliers have two grooves in their jaws to enable you to fold or roll a crimp into a compact shape.

Use a **hammer** to harden and flatten wire for strong connections. Any hammer with a flat head will work, as long as the head is free of nicks that could mar your metal. The lightweight ballpeen hammer shown here is one of the most commonly used hammers for jewelry making.

On **diagonal wire cutters**, the outside (back) of the blades meets squarely for a flat-cut surface. The inside (front) of the blades makes a pointed cut.

A **bench block** provides a hard, smooth surface on which to hammer your pieces. An anvil is similarly hard but has different surfaces, such as a tapered horn, to help forge wire into different shapes.

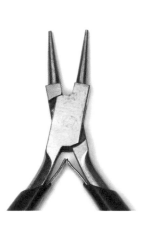

Roundnose pliers have smooth, tapered, conical jaws used to form loops. The closer to the tip you work, the smaller the loop will be.

A **mandrel** is used to shape wire into uniform loops and angles, or to measure wire for rings or jewelry components.

Metal files are used to refine and shape the edges of metal and wire surfaces.

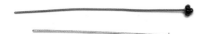

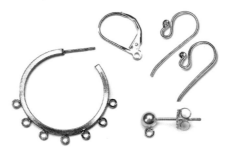

A **head pin** looks like a long, thick, blunt sewing pin. It has a flat or decorative head on one end to keep the beads in place. Head pins come in different diameters, or gauges, and lengths ranging from 1–3 in. (2.5–7.6cm).

Earring wires come in a huge variety of metals and styles, including lever-back, French hook, post, and hoop. You will almost always want a loop on earring findings so you can attach beads.

Findings like filigree and chandelier components, tube beads, multi-strand spacer bars, and connectors let you connect and position the elements of your jewelry.

A **jump ring** is used to connect two loops or make chain mail. It is a small wire circle or oval that is either soldered or comes with a split that you can open and close.

Use **bead caps** to enclose or set off large-hole beads. Bead caps come in many different shapes and styles.

Flexible beading wire consists of fine wires that have been twisted or braided together, and it comes in a variety of sizes. Use thicker varieties (.018 or .019) when stringing heavy beads, and use thinner varieties (.014 or .015) for stringing smaller beads and pearls.

Crimp beads are small, large-holed, thin-walled metal beads designed to be flattened or crimped into a tight roll. Use them when stringing jewelry on flexible beading wire.

Spacers are small beads used between larger beads to space the beads' placement.

Ribbon elastic is usually used for stretchy, slip-on bracelets with no clasp or closure that must expand to fit over the wearer's hand. You may need to use a beading needle to string your beads on the elastic.

Bead tips are small metal beads primarily used to link a strand of beads on a cord to a clasp. They come in a clamshell or basket shape. Clamshell bead tips close over a knot to hide it. The knot rests against the basket in basket-shaped bead tips.

Clasps come in many sizes and shapes. Some of the most common are the toggle, the lobster claw, the magnetic, the S-hook, the box, the slide, and the hook and eye.

Wire is used to make loops or to wrap beads. The smaller the gauge, the thicker the wire.

Crystals

for Special Occasions

Twinkling, light, and airy

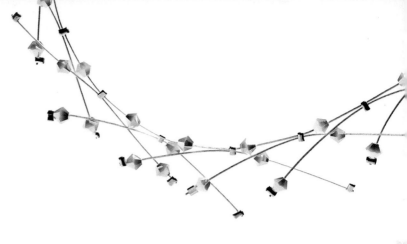

Crimp your style with sparkling possibilities

by Mia Gofar

This ethereal look comes from a lot of down-to-earth crimping. Everything about the necklace, bracelet, and earring set can be altered to fit your style — just change the size of the crystals or the length of the beading wire pieces.

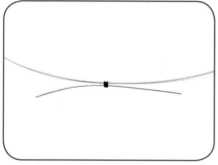

1 necklace • **a** Cut a piece of beading wire (Basics, p. 5). Center a crimp bead.

b Cut a 2-in. (5cm) piece of beading wire. String it through the crimp bead so the bead is centered on the short wire. Flatten the crimp bead (Basics).

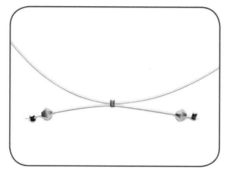

2 On each end of the short wire, string a bicone crystal and a crimp bead. Flatten the crimp beads.

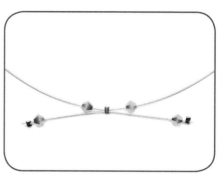

3 On each end of the long wire, string a bicone.

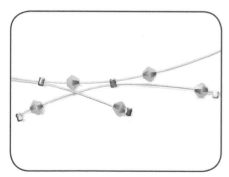

4 On each end of the long wire, string a crimp bead about ½ in. (1.3cm) from the last crimp bead strung. Follow steps 1b, 2, and 3. Repeat until the short-wire segments reach the finished length. Check the fit. Allowing 1 in. (2.5cm) for the finishing, trim the long wire to the finished length.

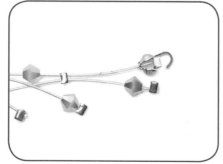

5 On each end of the long wire, string a bead tip and a crimp bead. Flatten the crimp bead. Use chainnose pliers to close the bead tip over the crimp.

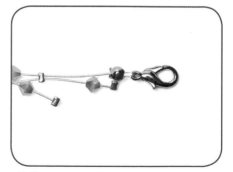

6 On one end, string a lobster claw clasp on the loop of the bead tip. Use chainnose pliers to close the loop. Repeat on the other end, substituting a split ring for the clasp.

necklace 18 in. (46cm)
- ◆ **80-92** 4mm bicone crystals
- ◆ flexible beading wire, .018 or .019
- ◆ 6mm split ring
- ◆ **2** bead tips, clamshell style
- ◆ **80-92** crimp beads
- ◆ lobster claw clasp
- ◆ chainnose pliers
- ◆ diagonal wire cutters

bracelet
- ◆ **26-30** 4mm bicone crystals
- ◆ flexible beading wire, .018 or .019
- ◆ **2** bead tips, clamshell style
- ◆ **26-30** crimp beads
- ◆ magnetic clasp
- ◆ chainnose pliers
- ◆ diagonal wire cutters

earrings
- ◆ **10** 4mm bicone crystals
- ◆ flexible beading wire, .018 or .019
- ◆ **2** 2-in. (5cm) head pins
- ◆ **12** crimp beads
- ◆ pair of earring wires
- ◆ chainnose pliers
- ◆ diagonal wire cutters
- ◆ roundnose pliers

bracelet • Follow the necklace instructions, but cut the short wires ¾ in. (1.9cm) long, space the crimp beads ¼ in. (6mm) apart on the longer wire, and substitute a magnetic clasp for the lobster claw clasp and split ring.

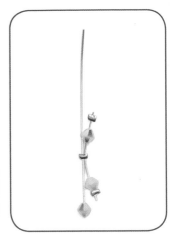

1 earrings • On a head pin, string a bicone crystal.

2a String a crimp bead and position it ½ in. (1.3cm) from the bicone.
b Cut a ½-in. (1.3cm) piece of beading wire. String it through the crimp bead so the bead is centered. Flatten the crimp bead (Basics). Follow necklace step 2.

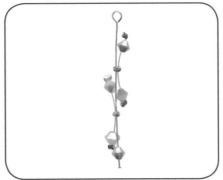

3 On the head pin, string a crimp bead ½ in. (1.3cm) from the last crimp bead strung. Repeat earring step 2b.

4 Make a plain loop (Basics).

5 Open the loop of an earring wire (Basics). Attach the dangle and close the loop. Make a second earring to match the first.

Tips

- Because the beading wire is exposed, Mia used .018 24k-plated gold beading wire and .019 sterling silver. For a stiffer bracelet, use heavier (.024) beading wire.
- The gold necklace is made with Swarovski Elements olivine crystals; the silver necklace is made with white alabaster AB2X.

- To save time, cut all of the short pieces of wire first. For the necklace, you'll need 27 to 35 short pieces; for the bracelet, cut 13 to 15.

Diamonds and pearls

Pair crystals and pearls for twice the dazzling elegance

by Patricia Bartlein

For a quick, dressy accent, try a crystal-and-pearl bracelet. Crystal chaton montées have four holes for stringing, so this sparkling piece will lie flat when you wear it.

Supplies

- ◆ **5** 8mm two-strand crystal chaton montées
- ◆ **4–6** 10mm round pearls
- ◆ **24–28** 4mm round pearls
- ◆ **24–28** 3mm bicone crystals
- ◆ flexible beading wire, .012 or .013
- ◆ **4** crimp beads
- ◆ two-strand clasp
- ◆ chainnose or crimping pliers
- ◆ diagonal wire cutters

Tip

To make sure that the bracelet lies flat, try not to cross the two wires when you're stringing.

1 Cut two pieces of beading wire (Basics, p. 5). On each wire, string: bicone crystal, 4mm pearl, corresponding holes of a chaton montée, 4mm pearl, bicone. Center the beads.

2 On each side, over both ends, string a 10mm pearl.

3 Repeat the patterns in steps 1 and 2 until the bracelet is within 1 in. (2.5cm) of the finished length.

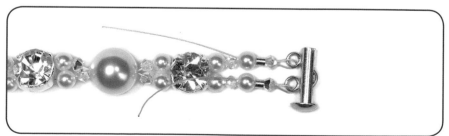

4 On each end, string a 4mm pearl, a crimp bead, a bicone, and the corresponding loop of half of the clasp. Check the fit, and add or remove beads from each end if necessary. Go back through the beads just strung and tighten the wires. Crimp the crimp beads (Basics) and trim the excess wire.

Channel the brilliance of crystals

Link crystal and channel-set components to make a vivid necklace and earrings

by Irina Miech

Make wrapped loops to connect a spectrum of bicone and channel-set crystals. Add chain, and this long necklace and earrings will put you on the path to smart fashion.

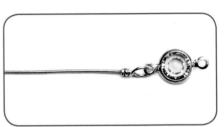

1 necklace • Cut a 2-in. (5cm) piece of wire. Make the first half of a wrapped loop (Basics, p. 5) on one end. String a loop of a channel-set component and complete the wraps.

2 Cut a 2-in. piece of wire. Make the first half of a wrapped loop. Attach the component's remaining loop and complete the wraps.

3 On each wire, string a bicone crystal and make the first half of a wrapped loop.

Supplies

necklace
- **28** 4mm bicone crystals, in six colors
- **21** 5mm two-loop channel-set components, in six colors
- 56 in. (1.4m) 24-gauge half-hard wire
- 2 ft. (61cm) chain, 4–6mm links
- chainnose pliers
- diagonal wire cutters
- roundnose pliers

earrings
- **6** 4mm bicone crystals, in three colors
- **6** 5mm one-loop channel-set components, in three colors
- 1 ft. (30cm) 24-gauge half-hard wire
- 7 in. (18cm) chain, 4–6mm links
- **2** 4–5mm jump rings
- pair of earring wires
- chainnose pliers
- diagonal wire cutters
- roundnose pliers

4 On each loop, string a component's loop and complete the wraps.

5a On each end, repeat steps 2 and 3.
5b Follow steps 1 through 5a to make seven crystal strands.

6 Decide how long you want your necklace to be. Subtract 16 in. (41cm) and cut a piece of chain to that length. Cut the chain into seven equal pieces. On each end of one crystal strand, attach a chain and complete the wraps. Attach the remaining crystal strands and chains, alternating each. Connect the last crystal strand to the first chain segment.

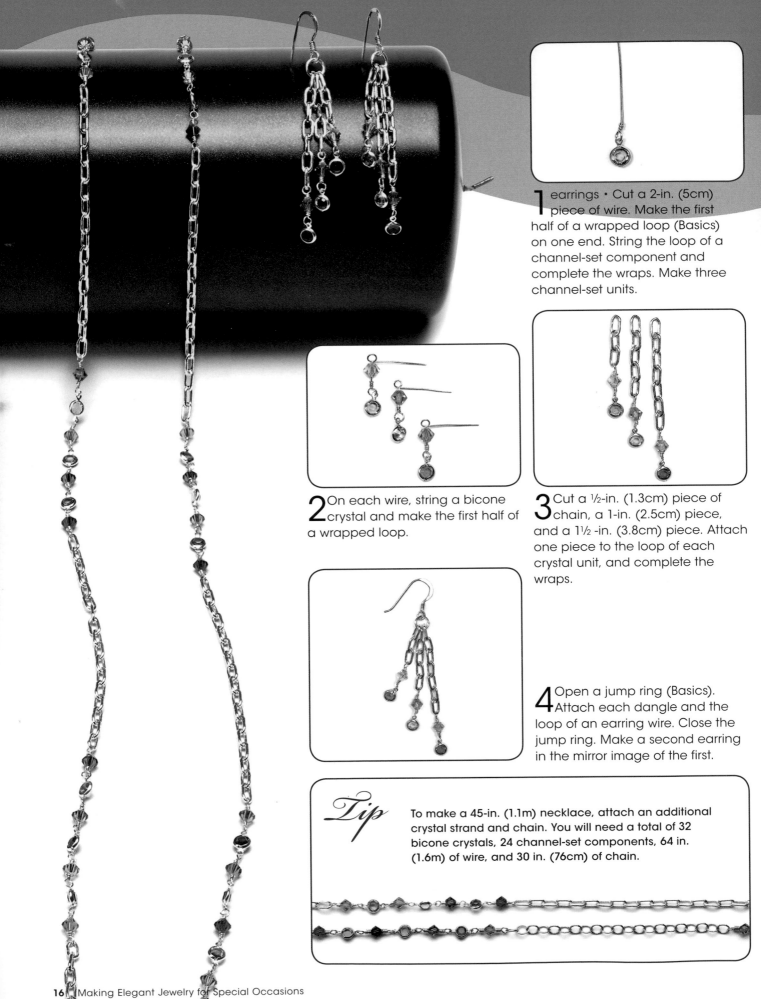

1 earrings • Cut a 2-in. (5cm) piece of wire. Make the first half of a wrapped loop (Basics) on one end. String the loop of a channel-set component and complete the wraps. Make three channel-set units.

2 On each wire, string a bicone crystal and make the first half of a wrapped loop.

3 Cut a ½-in. (1.3cm) piece of chain, a 1-in. (2.5cm) piece, and a 1½ -in. (3.8cm) piece. Attach one piece to the loop of each crystal unit, and complete the wraps.

4 Open a jump ring (Basics). Attach each dangle and the loop of an earring wire. Close the jump ring. Make a second earring in the mirror image of the first.

Tip

To make a 45-in. (1.1m) necklace, attach an additional crystal strand and chain. You will need a total of 32 bicone crystals, 24 channel-set components, 64 in. (1.6m) of wire, and 30 in. (76cm) of chain.

Clear winner

Favorite colors meet in a sparkling design

by Cathy Jakicic

The classic look for this necklace comes from the elegant drape of the layered strands. One of the most popular colors of CRYSTALLIZED™ - *Swarovski Elements* crystals, "crystal," is combined with two other popular colors — "Montana" and "tanzanite" — to form a glittering collar.

1 necklace • Cut three pieces of beading wire, each 38–48 in. (.97–1.2m) long. On one wire, center a pendant.

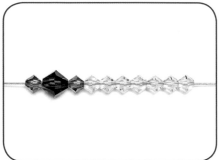

2 On each end, string a 4mm tanzanite bicone, a 6mm Montana bicone, and a tanzanite. String 4mm crystal bicones until the strand is within ½ in. (1.3cm) of the finished length.

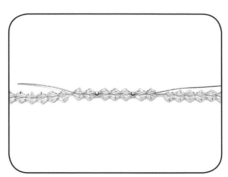

3 On one end, string a crimp bead, three crystal bicones, and a crimp bead. String the other end through the beads just strung, plus a few more. Tighten the wire and flatten the crimp beads (Basics, p. 5). Trim the excess wire.

4 On the second wire, string a tanzanite, a Montana, a tanzanite, and 13 crystal bicones. Repeat until the strand is within ½ in. (1.3cm) of the finished length. Follow step 3 to finish the strand.

On the third wire, string crystal bicones until the strand is within ½ in. (1.3cm) of the finished length Follow step 3 to finish the strand.

5 Looping one end of each strand over your index fingers, twist the strands together. Open a pearl shortener and attach the ends of the twisted strands.

1 earrings • On a head pin, string four 4mm crystal bicones. Make the first half of a wrapped loop (Basics). On a head pin, string a 4mm tanzanite bicone and a 6mm Montana bicone. Using the largest part of your roundnose pliers, make a plain loop (Basics).

Supplies

necklace (32 in./81cm; with pearl shortener 14 in./36cm)

- ◆ 30mm avant-garde pendant, crystal
- ◆ **16–20** 6mm bicone crystals, Montana
- ◆ **616–660** (5 gross) 4mm bicone crystals, crystal
- ◆ **32–40** 4mm bicone crystals, tanzanite
- ◆ flexible beading wire, .014 or .015
- ◆ pearl shortener
- ◆ **6** crimp beads
- ◆ chainnose pliers
- ◆ diagonal wire cutters

earrings

- ◆ **2** 6mm bicone crystals, Montana
- ◆ **8** 4mm bicone crystals, crystal
- ◆ **2** 4mm bicone crystals, tanzanite
- ◆ **4** 1½-in. (3.8cm) head pins
- ◆ pair of square earring hoops with one loop
- ◆ chainnose pliers
- ◆ diagonal wire cutters
- ◆ roundnose pliers

2 Attach the four-crystal unit to the loop of an earring hoop. Complete the wraps.

3 String the two-crystal unit over the hoop. Make a second earring to match the first.

Design alternative

Blues sing a happy note when played together. Combine Montana, tanzanite, and indicolite dangles on a simple chain for striking results.

Tips

• Wear one or all of the necklace strands without the pearl shortener for a long, swingy look.
• Remove the Montana/tanzanite dangle from the earrings and they'll match nearly everything in your wardrobe.
• To save money, buy large quantities of crystals from vendors that sell them by the gross.

An intricate choker is perfect
for a formal occasion

by Kathie Scrimgeour

For a

special day

To accessorize a picture-perfect bride on her special day, incorporate distinctive materials, including beading chain, specialty tube beads, and crystals. Use small tube beads and clear crystals for a wedding, or try larger tube beads and darker crystals for a dressy necklace that's less formal.

1 Decide how long you want your necklace to be. (These necklaces are 17 in./43cm.) Double that measurement, add 12 in. (30cm), and cut two pieces of beading wire to that length. Cut two pieces of beading chain, each 1 in. (2.5cm) longer than the finished length.

On each wire, string one side of an X-tube bead. Center the bead on the wires.

Supplies

- **15–17** 5–12mm X-tube beads
- **32–36** 9 x 1.5mm two-strand curved tube beads
- **30–34** 4mm bicone crystals
- **40–44** 3mm bicone crystals
- **8** 4mm round beads
- **152–176** 3mm round beads
- flexible beading wire, .010 or .012
- **36–40 in.** (.9–1m) beading chain
- **2** crimp beads
- **4** crimp covers
- toggle clasp
- chainnose pliers
- diagonal wire cutters
- crimping pliers (optional)

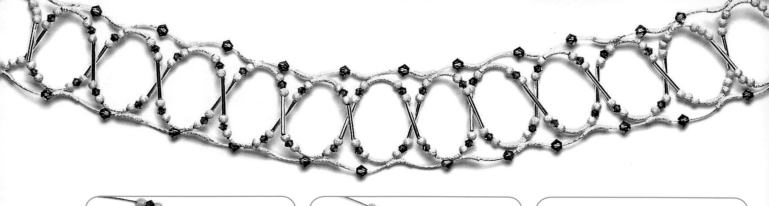

2 On each end of each wire, string: 3mm round bead, 3mm bicone crystal, 3mm round, one side of a curved tube bead, 3mm round, 3mm bicone, 3mm round, one side of an X tube. Repeat until the strands are within 8 in. (20cm) of the finished length.

3 On each end of each wire, string: three 3mm rounds, one side of a curved tube, three 3mm rounds, one side of an X tube. Repeat until the strands are within 3 in. (7.6cm) of the finished length. End with three 3mm rounds.

4 On each side, over both wires, string four 4mm round beads, a crimp bead, and half of a clasp. Check the fit, and add or remove beads from each end if necessary. Go back through the beads just strung and tighten the wires, leaving approximately ³/₈ in. (1cm) between the crimp bead and the clasp. Crimp the crimp bead (Basics, p. 5) and trim the excess wire.

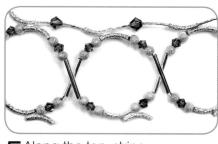

5 Along the top, string beading chain through the remaining side of a curved tube, and then string a 4mm bicone crystal. Repeat until you've strung all the curved tubes along the top.

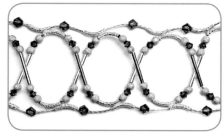

6 Along the bottom, string the curved tubes and crystals with the remaining piece of beading chain.

Tip

To make sure that the necklace curves properly, string the two-strand curved tube beads in the same direction.

7 On each end, use chainnose pliers to close a crimp cover over the crimp bead and chains. Close an additional crimp cover over the chains and the exposed beading wire. Trim the excess chain.

Monet's colors bloom

in a crystal necklace

**WireLace provides
a flexible landscape
for a pastel palette**

by Linda Hartung

Capture the colors of Monet's *Water Lilies* in this clever necklace, with aqua, green, and lavender crystals paired with teal WireLace. Or, create your own garden with seasonal colors.

✒ Supplies

- **6** 14mm octagonal crystals, in one or two colors
- **36–40** 6mm saucer crystals, top drilled
- **36–40** 6mm bicone crystals, top drilled
- 3g 13º seed beads
- silver-plated flexible beading wire, .018
- 1 yd. (.9m) WireLace
- **2** 4mm bell end caps
- **4** 2mm crimp beads
- teardrop-shaped clasp
- 8 x 4.8mm teardrop-shaped crystal for clasp
- chainnose pliers
- diagonal wire cutters
- crimping pliers (optional)
- G-S Hypo cement

SUPPLY NOTES
• Use silver-plated beading wire so it disappears in the focal piece. Also, if the wire is thicker than .018, the center part of the flower won't work.
• The thickness of the WireLace and the hole size of some crystals vary. When shopping for materials, make sure the WireLace will go through the crystals.

1 Cut a 1-yd. (.9m) piece of WireLace. (This necklace is 17 in./43cm.) Twist each end. Trim the ends at an angle to form a tip, and apply glue to each tip. Let glue dry.

2 Center an octagonal crystal on the WireLace.

3 a Cut a 30-in. (76cm) piece of beading wire. String the wire through the octagonal crystal, being careful not to snag the WireLace. Pull the wire through until one side is about 2 in. (5cm) longer than the other.

b On the longer side, string an alternating pattern of six top-drilled bicone crystals and five octagons. If you are using two colors of octagons, alternate colors.

4 String the beaded end of the wire through the centered octagon, forming a loop. String the wire through all the crystals and back through the centered octagon.

5 Adjust the wire so it's approximately the same length on both sides (within 2 in./5cm). Tighten the wire and arrange the crystals to form a flower. Tighten the wire again. String a crimp bead on each end and crimp the crimp beads (Basics, p. 5) as close to the crystal flower as possible.

6 On each end of the WireLace, string pairs of bicones 1½ in. (3.8cm) apart until the strand is within 1 in. (2.5cm) of the desired length.

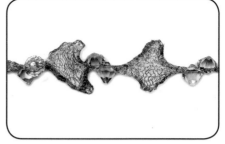

7 Gently pull the sides of the WireLace apart between each crystal pair and after the last pair.

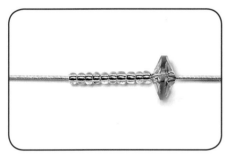

8 On each end of the wire, string 10 13º seed beads and a saucer crystal.

9 On each side, string each end of the wire through the first section of WireLace.

10 On each end of the wire, string a saucer, 20 13ºs, a saucer, and the next section of WireLace. Repeat until the wire has passed between the last set of crystal pairs.

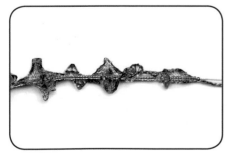

11 Check the fit, and add or remove beads if necessary. On each end of the wire, string a saucer and 10 13ºs. On each side, string a crimp bead over both the wire and the WireLace. Crimp the crimp bead.

12 Apply glue to the inside of an end cap, and attach it to one end of the strand. Repeat on the other end.

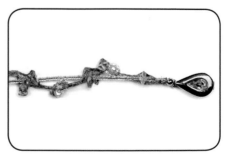

13 On each end, open the loop of the end cap and attach half of the clasp.

A dramatic
crystal filigree
component anchors
softly draped chains

by Arleen Bejerano

Focus on simple

When you have a beautiful focal point, it's smart to keep things simple, but never ordinary. This contemporary necklace has an off-center centerpiece, delicate chains, and bicones of coordinating colors.

elegance

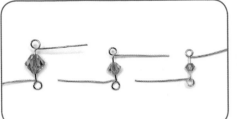  

1 necklace • Cut a 2½-in. (6.4cm) piece of wire. Make the first half of a wrapped loop (Basics, p. 5) on one end. String a large bicone crystal. Make the first half of a wrapped loop. Make six large-bicone units, 11 medium-bicone units, and three small-bicone units.

2 Cut a 10–14-in. (25–36cm) piece of chain, depending on the desired length of your necklace. (These necklaces are 15 in./38cm and use a 10-in./25cm chain.) Open two 2mm jump rings (Basics) and attach each end of the chain and a loop of the filigree component as shown. Close the jump rings.

3 String a 4mm jump ring through the two center links of the chain.

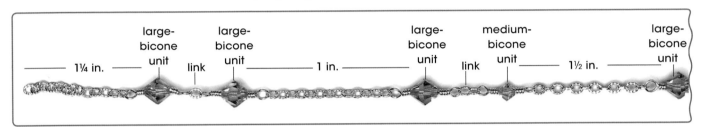

large-bicone unit — large-bicone unit — link — 1¼ in. — large-bicone unit — link — medium-bicone unit — 1½ in. — large-bicone unit — 1 in.

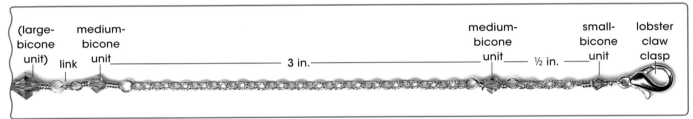

(large-bicone unit) — link — medium-bicone unit — 3 in. — medium-bicone unit — ½ in. — small-bicone unit — lobster claw clasp

4 To make the longest strand: Cut chains to the lengths shown. Attach components as shown. Attach a lobster claw clasp to the end loop of the small-bicone unit. Complete the wraps.

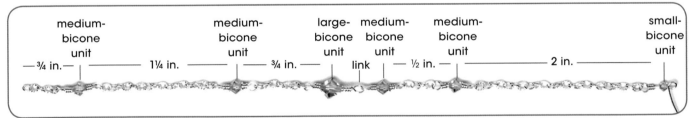

medium-bicone unit — ¾ in. — medium-bicone unit — 1¼ in. — large-bicone unit — ¾ in. — medium-bicone unit — link — medium-bicone unit — ½ in. — small-bicone unit — 2 in.

5 To make the shortest strand: Cut chains to the lengths shown. Attach components as shown. Complete the wraps, leaving the end loop of the small-bicone unit open.

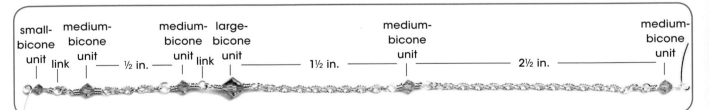

small-bicone unit — link — medium-bicone unit — ½ in. — medium-bicone unit — link — large-bicone unit — 1½ in. — medium-bicone unit — 2½ in. — medium-bicone unit

6 To make the middle strand: Cut chains to the lengths shown. Attach components as shown. Complete the wraps, leaving the end loops open.

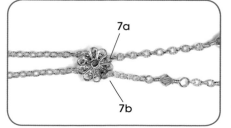

Supplies

necklace

- crystal filigree component (25mm component from Chic Beads, chicbeads.com; 11mm component from Jewelry Supply Inc., jewelrysupply.com)
- **6** 8–10mm bicone crystals
- **11** 4–8mm bicone crystals
- **3** 3–4mm bicone crystals
- 45–50 in. (1.1–1.3m) 24-gauge half-hard wire
- 1 yd. (.9m) cable chain, 3–4mm links
- **4** 2mm jump rings
- lobster claw clasp and 4mm jump ring
- chainnose pliers
- diagonal wire cutters
- roundnose pliers

earrings

- **2** crystal filigree components (Jewelry Supply Inc., jewelrysupply.com)
- **2** 8mm bicone crystals
- 2 in. (5cm) cable chain, 3–4mm links
- **2** 2-in. (5cm) head pins
- **4** 2mm jump rings
- pair of earring posts with ear nuts
- chainnose pliers
- diagonal wire cutters
- roundnose pliers

7 a Use a 2mm jump ring to attach the longest strand and a loop of the filigree component.

b Use a 2mm jump ring to attach the end link of the shortest strand and a loop of the filigree component.

8 Attach the small-bicone unit of the middle strand to the filigree-component loop in step 7b. Complete the wraps.

9 Attach the small-bicone unit of the shortest strand to the loop of the medium-bicone unit of the longest strand nearest the clasp. Complete the wraps.

10 Attach the medium-bicone unit of the middle strand to the longest strand approximately 2½ in. (6.4cm) from the clasp. Complete the wraps.

1 earrings • String a large bicone crystal on a head pin. Make the first half of a wrapped loop (Basics). Cut a 1-in. (2.5cm) piece of chain.

2 Open a 2mm jump ring (Basics). Attach the chain and a filigree component. Close the jump ring. Attach the bicone unit to the remaining end of the chain. Complete the wraps.

3 Use a jump ring to attach the dangle and the loop of an earring post. Make a second earring to match the first.

Diamond
alternative

Chunky crystals are almost better than the real thing

by Jenny Van

Crystals are always a pretty and affordable alternative to diamonds. These earrings use galactic crystals in "crystal silver shade" for a hint of grey, but if you're a purist, you can get them in "crystal" for a pristine sparkle.

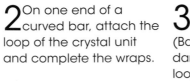

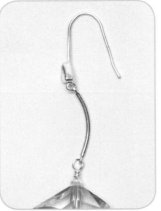

1 On a head pin, string a bicone crystal, a galactic crystal, and a bicone. Make the first half of a wrapped loop (Basics, p. 5).

2 On one end of a curved bar, attach the loop of the crystal unit and complete the wraps.

3 Open the loop of a decorative earring wire (Basics). Attach the dangle and close the loop. Make a second earring to match the first.

Supplies

- **2** 19mm galactic crystals
- **4** 3mm bicone crystals
- **2** 14mm curved bars (removed from bar-and-link chain)
- **2** 1½-in. (3.8cm) head pins
- pair of decorative earring wires
- chainnose pliers
- diagonal wire cutters
- roundnose pliers

Light
and lively

by Karin Buckingham

Make a lightweight silver and crystal necklace with matching earrings

1 necklace • Determine the finished length of your necklace. Cut a piece of beading chain to that length, and two more, each 2 in. (5cm) longer than the previous.

String a micro crimp, one to three crystals, and a micro crimp on the shortest strand. Continue stringing sets of crystals with micro crimps on either side.

2 Space each grouping as desired and flatten each crimp bead (Basics, p. 5).

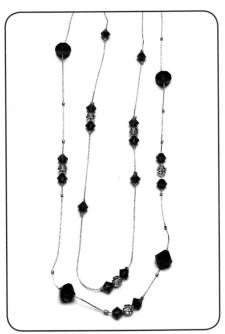

3 Plan your second strand by staggering the placement of the crystals in comparison with the first strand. Flatten the crimp beads. Repeat for the third strand.

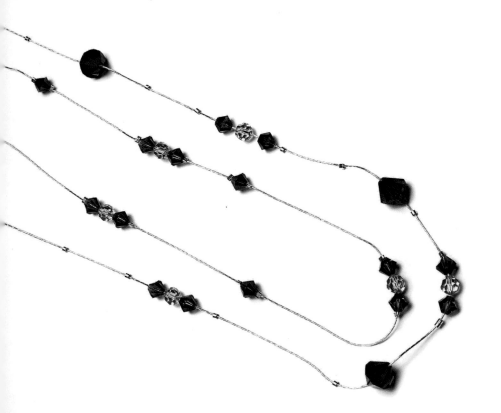

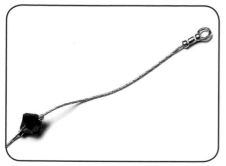

4 Slide a crimp-end loop onto one end of one chain. Flatten the middle crimp section with chainnose pliers. Repeat on ends of all chain.

5 Open a jump ring (Basics) and slide on the clasp and three crimp-end loops. Close the jump ring. Repeat on the other end with just the crimp ends.

Supplies

necklace 18 in. (46cm)

◆ 5 ft. (1.5m) beading chain, 0.6mm
◆ **4** or more 10mm bicone crystals
◆ **33** or more 6mm bicone crystals, in **2** colors
◆ **11** or more 6mm round crystals
◆ **50** or more micro crimps
◆ **6** crimp ends (loop style), 0.8mm
◆ **2** 4–5mm jump rings
◆ lobster claw clasp with jump ring
◆ chainnose pliers
◆ diagonal wire cutters

earrings

◆ 3 in. (7.6cm) or more beading chain, 0.6mm
◆ crystals left over from necklace
◆ **2** crimp ends (loop style), 0.8mm
◆ **2** micro crimps

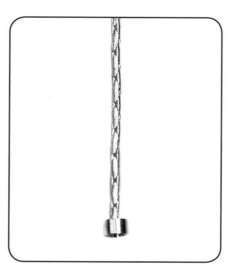

1 earrings • Determine the finished length of your earrings. (These are 1½ in./3.8cm.) Cut a piece of beading chain to that length. String a micro crimp. Flatten the crimp bead at the end of the chain.

2 String crystals as desired.

3 Slide a crimp-end loop onto the other end of the chain. Flatten the middle section with chainnose pliers.

4 Open an earring wire and attach the crimp-end loop. Close the earring wire. Make a second earring to match the first.

Extended
style

One long strand glimmers without end

by Angie D'Amato

This inexpensive necklace is a snap to string. The metallic finish on the fire-polished crystals glams up this long look. Wear the necklace as one long strand, or loop it around your neck for multistrand magic. Or, try a hinged twister clasp to convert this continuous loop into a shorter necklace. Ease a few stretchy strands on your wrist as glitzy companions.

1 necklace • Cut a piece of beading wire (Basics, p. 5). String crystals until the strand is within 1 in. (2.5cm) of the finished length.

2 On one end, string a crimp bead, a crystal, and a crimp bead.

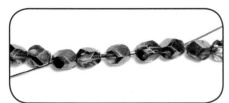

3 String the other end through the last few beads strung. Check the fit, and add or remove beads if necessary. Tighten the wire and crimp the crimp beads (Basics). Trim the excess wire.

Tips

• For speedy stringing, thread the beading wire through the 8mm beads while they're still on their original string. When you've strung enough beads on the beading wire, pull out the original string.
• To make sure the necklace loops around multiple times, avoid overtightening the wire in step 3.

1 bracelet • Decide how long you want your bracelet to be, add 3 in. (7.6cm), and cut a piece of ribbon elastic to that length. String beads until the bracelet is the finished length.

2 Tie a square or surgeon's knot (Basics). Trim the ends and glue the knot.

Supplies

necklace 64 in. (1.6m)
- ◆ **4** 16-in. (41cm) strands 8mm Czech fire-polished crystals
- ◆ flexible beading wire, .018 or .019
- ◆ **2** crimp beads
- ◆ crimping pliers
- ◆ diagonal wire cutters

bracelet
- ◆ **18–24** 8mm glass beads per bracelet
- ◆ ribbon elastic
- ◆ G-S Hypo Cement

Design alternative

To add more dimension to your necklace, combine two or more shapes of Czech glass beads.

Pearls

for Special Occasions

Try your hand at something new

by Debbie Tuttle

Knot this time

New to knotting? You'll get into the rhythm of this knotted necklace project with just a little practice. The knots add a bit of length, so you may need to remove beads from opposite sides of the graduated strand before starting. Take your time tying knots; Debbie likes to take breaks rather than trying to finish in one sitting. If you're pressed for time, try a simpler version with bigger beads (like the ones on p. 40).

1 **necklace** • **a** Unwind a card of beading cord.
b On the end without the needle, string a bead tip and tie two overhand knots (Basics, p. 5), one on top of the other. Trim the excess cord and apply glue to the knot.

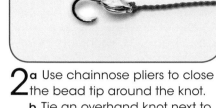

2 **a** Use chainnose pliers to close the bead tip around the knot.
b Tie an overhand knot next to the bead tip.

3 Starting from one end of a strand of graduated beads, string a bead and tie a knot. Repeat until the strand is symmetrical and within 1 in. (2.5cm) of the finished length. End with a knot. Repeat steps 1b and 2a.

4 On each end, close the loop of the bead tip. On one end, open a jump ring (Basics). Attach a lobster claw clasp and the bead tip's loop. Close the jump ring. Repeat on the other end, substituting a soldered jump ring for the clasp.

5 Trim the head from a head pin. Make a plain loop (Basics). String a bicone crystal, a bead, and a bicone. Make a plain loop. On another head pin, string a bicone, a bead, and a bicone. Make a plain loop.

6 Open each loop (Basics) of the two-loop bead unit. Attach the head-pin unit to one loop and the soldered jump ring to the other. Close the loops.

Supplies

necklace 17½ in. (44.5cm)
- 15–16-in. (38–41cm) strand 3–7mm graduated beads
- **4** 4mm bicone crystals
- card of beading cord with attached needle, size 4
- **2** 2-in. (5cm) head pins
- **2** 3–4mm jump rings
- **2** bead tips
- lobster claw clasp and soldered jump ring
- chainnose pliers
- diagonal wire cutters
- roundnose pliers
- G-S Hypo Cement
- awl (optional)

bracelet
- **32–38** 3–7mm graduated beads
- 4mm bicone crystal
- card of beading cord with attached needle, size 4
- 1¼ in. (3.2cm) chain, 4–6mm links
- 2-in. (5cm) head pin
- **2** 3–4mm jump rings
- **2** bead tips
- lobster claw clasp
- chainnose pliers
- diagonal wire cutters
- roundnose pliers
- G-S Hypo Cement
- awl (optional)

earrings
- **6** 3–7mm round beads, in graduated pairs
- **2** 4mm bicone crystals
- **2** 2-in. (5cm) head pins
- pair of earring wires
- chainnose pliers
- diagonal wire cutters
- roundnose pliers

1 bracelet • Follow steps 1 and 2 of the necklace. String three beads and tie an overhand knot (Basics). Alternate three beads and a knot until the bracelet is within 1 in. (2.5cm) of the finished length. End with a knot.

2 Repeat steps 1b and 2a of the necklace. On each end, close the loop of the bead tip. On one end, open a jump ring (Basics). Attach a lobster claw clasp and the bead tip's loop. Close the jump ring. Repeat on the other end, substituting a 1¼-in. (3.2cm) piece of chain for the clasp.

3 On a head pin, string two beads and a bicone crystal. Make the first half of a wrapped loop (Basics). Attach the end link of the chain and complete the wraps.

1 earrings • On a head pin, string three beads and a bicone crystal. Make a plain loop (Basics).

2 Open the loop of an earring wire (Basics). Attach the dangle and close the loop. Make a second earring to match the first.

Tip

For a quicker project and easier knotting, use bigger beads. String the thickest beading cord that will go through the beads.

Tip

To accurately place knots, use roundnose pliers or an awl to pull the knot close to the bead as you tighten it.

Design alternative

This version uses a strand of vintage crystals. Check estate sales and antique shops for graduated crystal necklaces that you can restring. Then, knot the crystals on a colorful cord that really makes them pop.

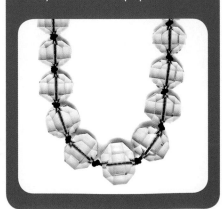

Pretty in pink and plum

Play up the beauty of a single blossom in a fresh necklace and earrings

by Lori Anderson

A Lucite flower forms the centerpiece of this lightweight necklace. Matte flowers are available in shades including tangerine, watermelon, and raspberry blush, offering you many options to accent a floral dress or make bridesmaids' jewelry. To complete the set without being too matchy-matchy, make earrings with a different kind of flower in a smaller size, but in the same shade.

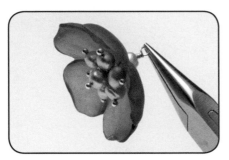

1 necklace • On a decorative head pin, string a pearl. Make a wrapped loop (Basics, p. 5). Make five or six pearl units.

2 On a decorative head pin, string a pearl and the pearl units.

3 String the Lucite flower and a pearl. Make a wrapped loop. Bend the loop upward.

4 Decide how long you want your necklace to be and cut a piece of chain to that length. Open a jump ring (Basics). About 1 in. (2.5cm) from the chain's center, attach a link and the pendant's loop. Close the jump ring.

Supplies

necklace 16-18 in. (41-46cm)
- 35–40mm Lucite flower, center drilled (The Beadin' Path, beadinpath.com)
- **8-9** 4-5mm round pearls
- 15-18 in. (38-46cm) cable chain, 3-5 mm links
- **7-8** 1½-in. (3.8cm) decorative head pins
- **2** 3-4mm jump rings
- lobster claw clasp
- chainnose pliers
- diagonal wire cutters
- roundnose pliers

earrings
- **2** 15-25mm Lucite flowers, center drilled (The Beadin' Path)
- **2** 4-5mm round pearls
- **2** 1½-in. (3.8cm) decorative head pins
- pair of earring wires
- chainnose pliers
- diagonal wire cutters
- roundnose pliers

5 Use a jump ring to attach the shorter end of the chain and a lobster claw clasp.

6 On a decorative head pin, string a pearl. Make the first half of a wrapped loop. Attach the dangle to the other end of the chain and complete the wraps.

Tip

For a simpler pendant, skip the pearl units and string a crystal rondelle in the center.

1 earrings • On a decorative head pin, string a pearl and a flower. Bend the head pin upward.

2 On the end of the head pin, make a wrapped loop (Basics).

3 Open the loop of an earring wire (Basics). Attach the dangle and close the loop. Make a second earring to match the first.

Tip

The number of pearl units you'll need for the center of the flower will depend on the pearls' size — the larger they are, the fewer units you'll need to make.

Design alternative

Make earrings with Lucite petal beads on hoops. The color will appear darker as you layer additional petals.

One superlong necklace
offers multiple looks

by Naomi Fujimoto

Pearls extend your
style options

By stringing crystals with four or five strands of pearls, you can make a necklace more than six feet long. And you won't need a clasp — simply wrap the pearls however the mood strikes you.

Supplies

necklace 75 in. (1.9m)
- **4–5** 16-in. (41cm) strands of 9–12mm pearls
- **140–160** 3mm crystals
- 3mm spacer
- flexible beading wire, .014 or .015
- **2** crimp beads
- chainnose or crimping pliers
- diagonal wire cutters

earrings
- **2** 9–12mm pearls
- **2** 3mm crystals
- **2** 1½-in. (3.8cm) head pins
- pair of earring wires
- chainnose pliers
- diagonal wire cutters
- roundnose pliers

1 necklace • Cut a piece of beading wire (Basics, p. 5). String a pearl and a crystal, repeating until the necklace is the finished length.

2 On each end, string a crystal and a crimp bead. String each end through a spacer in opposite directions. Go through the beads just strung. Tighten the wire and crimp the crimp bead (Basics). Trim the excess wire.

1 earrings • On a head pin, string a pearl and a crystal. Make a plain loop (Basics).

2 Open the loop of an earring wire (Basics) and attach the dangle. Close the loop. Make a second earring.

Tip

To lower your project costs, substitute 8º or 11º seed beads for the crystals.

Design alternative

Naomi used a strand of mixed quartz and chalcedony for a fun alternative to the sophisticated pearls. Make sure the stones aren't too big — six feet of beads can really weigh a girl down!

Pearl solitaire

A single pearl gives luminescent simplicity

by Kellie Sutton

Suspend a solitary pearl from a heart-shaped chandelier component for a no-frills necklace, then extend the chandelier theme by connecting components for dramatic earrings. You'll reach for this timeless set time and time again.

Supplies

necklace 20 in. (51cm)

- 12mm coin pearl
- 23mm chandelier component, with four loops
- 17–21 in. (43–53cm) cable chain, 3–5mm links
- 1½-in. (3.8cm) head pin
- **4** 3–4mm jump rings
- lobster claw clasp and soldered jump ring
- chainnose pliers
- diagonal wire cutters
- roundnose pliers

earrings

- **2** 12mm coin pearls
- **4** 23mm chandelier components, with four loops
- **2** 1½-in. (3.8cm) head pins
- **6** 3–4mm jump rings
- pair of decorative earring wires
- chainnose pliers
- diagonal wire cutters
- roundnose pliers

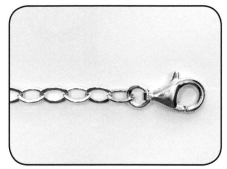

1 necklace • On a head pin, string a coin pearl. Make the first half of a wrapped loop (Basics, p. 5). Attach the single loop of a chandelier component as shown and complete the wraps.

2 Cut an 8–10-in. (20–25cm) piece of chain. Open a 3–4mm jump ring (Basics) and attach the chain and an outer loop of the chandelier component. Close the jump ring. Repeat on the other side of the component.

3 On one end, use a jump ring to attach the chain and a lobster claw clasp. Repeat on the other end, substituting a soldered jump ring for the clasp.

1 earrings • Repeat step 1 of the necklace. Open a jump ring (Basics) and attach an outer loop of a chandelier component and the corresponding loop of another component. Close the jump ring. Use jump rings to attach the remaining loops.

2 Open the loop of an earring wire (Basics). Attach the dangle and close the loop. Make a second earring to match the first.

Pastel
pearls

A pastel-hued necklace and earrings are a classic set

by Lindsay Mikulsky

Complement shimmering pink pearls with crystals. Add matching earrings for a set that gives you the best of both worlds.

SPECTACULAR OFFER!

P11145

$19.95 + FREE* = $35.70 ONLY $19.95

44% OFF

☑ **YES!** Send me 6 issues of *BeadStyle* magazine plus *Top 10 Quick Fixes for beaders* for only $19.95 That's a total savings of $15.75 off the annual newsstand rate!

Name _____

Address _____

City _____ State _____ Zip _____

☑ **YES!** I would like to receive a FREE e-mail newsletter, occasional news, updates, and special offers via e-mail from *BeadStyle* magazine.

E-mail _____

Or subscribe online at: **www.BeadStyleMag.com/Offer** and enter the code on the lower right.

L80BU

NO POSTAGE
NECESSARY
IF MAILED
IN THE
UNITED STATES

BUSINESS REPLY MAIL

FIRST-CLASS MAIL   PERMIT NO. 16   WAUKESHA, WI

POSTAGE WILL BE PAID BY ADDRESSEE

PO BOX 1612
WAUKESHA WI 53187-9950

1 necklace • Cut a piece of beading wire (Basics, p. 5). On the wire, center a rhinestone rondelle, a pearl, and a rhinestone rondelle.

2a On each end, string an alternating pattern of four gemstone rondelles and three pearls, stringing a spacer between each bead.

b String a rhinestone rondelle, a pearl, and a rhinestone rondelle.

c Repeat steps 2a and 2b on each end.

3 On each end, string a gemstone, a spacer, a pearl, and a spacer. Repeat until the necklace is within 1 in. (2.5cm) of the finished length.

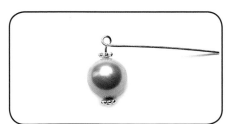

4 On each end, string two spacers, a crimp bead, two spacers, and a jump ring. Check the fit, and add or remove beads from each end if necessary. Go back through the last few beads strung and tighten the wire. Crimp the crimp bead (Basics) and trim the excess wire.

5 On one end, attach an S-hook clasp to the jump ring. Close one side of the clasp with chainnose pliers.

Supplies

necklace 28½ in. (72.4cm)
- 16-in. (41cm) strand 10mm pearls
- 16-in. (41cm) strand 8mm gemstone rondelles
- **10** 8mm rhinestone rondelles
- **60–80** 4mm flat spacers
- flexible beading wire, .014 or .015
- **2** crimp beads
- S-hook clasp with **2** soldered jump rings
- chainnose pliers
- diagonal wire cutters
- crimping pliers (optional)

earrings
- **2** 10mm pearls
- **4** 4mm flat spacers
- 3 in. (7.6cm) chain, 3–4mm links
- **2** 2-in. (5cm) head pins
- pair of earring wires
- chainnose pliers
- diagonal wire cutters
- roundnose pliers

Tip This design also works well as a choker. If you shorten the necklace, replace the pattern in step 2a with an alternating pattern of three gemstone rondelles and two pearls, stringing a spacer between each bead. This will keep the rhinestone rondelles near the front of the necklace.

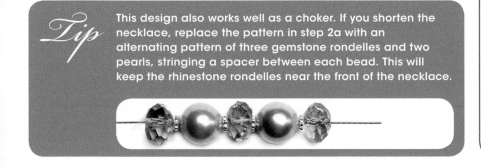

1 earrings • On a head pin, string a spacer, a pearl, and a spacer. Make the first half of a wrapped loop (Basics).

2 Cut a 1¼-in. (3.2cm) piece of chain. Attach the pearl unit to one end and complete the wraps.

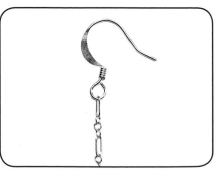

3 Open the loop of an earring wire (Basics). Attach the dangle and close the loop. Make a second earring to match the first.

Subtle&classic

A variety of colors brightens up a chain-and-pearl jewelry set

by Jackie Boettcher

Combine pearls and dainty bar-and-link chain for an elegant necklace, bracelet, and earrings. But remember — elegance should have a personality. Raise the stakes on this classic look by using pearls in many hues. The result will be a subtle spectrum that makes otherwise grown-up jewelry a little sassy.

1 necklace • On a head pin, string a pearl and a bead cap. Make a plain loop (Basics, p. 5). Make 12 pearl units.

center

2 Cut an 8½-in. (21.6cm) piece of chain with an even number of bars. (This will be the short strand of the necklace.) Open the loop of a pearl unit (Basics) and attach it to the center link. Close the loop. Repeat twice on each side, attaching a pearl unit every 1–1½ in. (2.5–3.8cm).

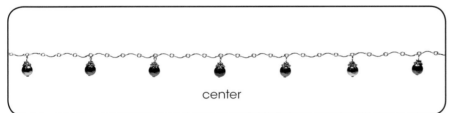

center

3 Decide how long you want your necklace to be and cut a piece of chain to that length. The chain should have an even number of bars. (This will be the long strand of the necklace.) Attach a pearl unit to the center link. Repeat three times on each side, attaching a pearl unit every 1–1½ in. (2.5–3.8cm).

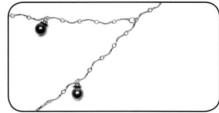

4 On each side, open a 4–5mm jump ring (Basics). Attach one end of the short chain to a link on the long chain about 2 in. (5cm) beyond the last pearl unit. Close the jump ring.

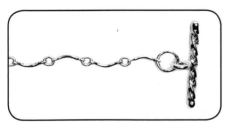

5 Check the fit, and trim chain from each end if necessary. On each end, use a 5–6mm jump ring to attach half of a clasp.

Supplies

necklace 16 in. (41cm)
- ◆ **12** 6mm pearls
- ◆ **12** 5–6mm bead caps
- ◆ 24–28 in. (61–71cm) bar-and-link chain, 7–10mm bars
- ◆ **12** 1-in. (2.5cm) head pins
- ◆ **2** 5–6mm jump rings
- ◆ **2** 4–5mm jump rings
- ◆ toggle clasp
- ◆ chainnose pliers
- ◆ diagonal wire cutters
- ◆ roundnose pliers

bracelet
- ◆ **5** 6mm pearls
- ◆ **5** 5–6mm bead caps
- ◆ 18–24 in. (46–61cm) bar-and-link chain, 7–10mm bars
- ◆ **5** 1-in. (2.5cm) head pins
- ◆ **2** 4–6mm jump rings
- ◆ lobster claw clasp and soldered jump ring
- ◆ chainnose pliers
- ◆ diagonal wire cutters
- ◆ roundnose pliers

earrings
- ◆ **6** 6mm pearls
- ◆ 3 in. (7.6cm) bar-and-link chain, 7–10mm bars
- ◆ **6** 1-in. (2.5cm) head pins
- ◆ **6** 3–4mm jump rings
- ◆ **2** three-to-one connectors or three-loop chandelier findings
- ◆ pair of earring wires
- ◆ chainnose pliers
- ◆ diagonal wire cutters
- ◆ roundnose pliers

1 bracelet • On a head pin, string a pearl and a bead cap. Using the largest part of your roundnose pliers, make a plain loop (Basics). Make five pearl units.

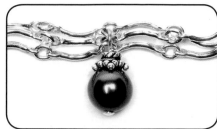

2 Decide how long you want your bracelet to be and cut three pieces of chain to that length. (Each chain should have an even number of bars.) Open the loop of a pearl unit (Basics) and attach it to the center link of all three chains.

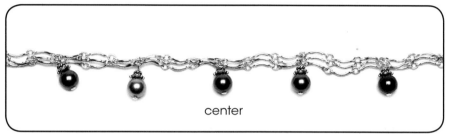

center

3 On each side, attach a pearl unit to all three chains 1 in. (2.5cm) from the center. Repeat.

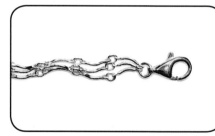

4 On one end, open a jump ring (Basics) and attach a lobster claw clasp. Close the jump ring. Repeat on the other end, substituting a soldered jump ring for the lobster claw clasp.

1 earrings • On a head pin, string a pearl and make a plain loop (Basics). Make three pearl units.

2 Cut three bars of chain. Open the loop of a pearl unit (Basics) and attach it to one end of a bar. Close the loop. Repeat with the remaining pearl units.

3 Open a jump ring (Basics) and attach a bar to the loop of a connector or chandelier finding. Close the jump ring. Repeat with the remaining bars.

4 Open the loop of an earring wire (Basics) and attach the dangle. Close the loop. Make a second earring to match the first.

Design alternative

For an extra challenge, try substituting simple chain mail for bar-and-link chain. Using 5mm jump rings, make stacks of three jump rings and connect the stacks with a single jump ring.

Small touches add
charm

Petal bead caps give a floral effect to a classic look

by Irina Miech

The sterling silver buds strung on this bracelet are elegant accents to a quick and easy project. This piece is sure to be a wardrobe perennial — or a great gift.

Supplies

bracelet
- ◆ **19–23** 10mm glass pearls
- ◆ **2** 3mm bicone crystals
- ◆ **2** 12mm petal bead caps
- ◆ flexible beading wire, .014 or .015
- ◆ **2** crimp beads
- ◆ toggle clasp
- ◆ chainnose or crimping pliers
- ◆ diagonal wire cutters

1 Cut a piece of beading wire (Basics, p. 5). Center pearls on the wire until the strand is within 1½ in. (3.8cm) of the finished length.

2 On each end, string a bead cap.

3 On each end, string a 3mm bicone crystal, a crimp bead, and half of a clasp. Check the fit, and add or remove beads if necessary. Go back through the last few beads strung and tighten the wire. Crimp the crimp bead (Basics) and trim the excess wire.

Pearls
and
chain

An asymetrical
necklace takes pearls
out of the classic realm

by Sara Strauss

Even though pearls speak
to tradition, the style of
this necklace is anything
but classic. Try this
asymmetrical piece with
brightly colored pearls.
Or create a version with
clear round crystals and
clear briolettes to make this
see-through jewelry trend
your own.

Supplies

necklace

- **2** 15–20mm briolettes
- **9–11** 6–9mm pearls
- 15–17 in. (38–43cm) 24-gauge half-hard wire
- 28–35 in. (71–89cm) chain, 2–3mm links
- 6–7mm jump ring
- **2** 4mm jump rings
- lobster claw clasp and soldered jump ring
- chainnose pliers
- diagonal wire cutters
- roundnose pliers

earrings

- **2** 6–9mm pearls
- 5–8 in. (13–20cm) chain, 2–3mm links
- **2** 1½-in. (3.8cm) head pins
- pair of earring wires
- chainnose pliers
- diagonal wire cutters
- roundnose pliers

1 necklace · Cut a 1-in. (2.5cm) piece of wire. Make a plain loop (Basics, p. 5) on one end. String a pearl and make a plain loop. Make nine to 11 pearl units.

2 Cut a 3-in. (7.6cm) piece of wire. String a briolette and make a set of wraps above it (Basics). Make the first half of a wrapped loop (Basics) above the wraps. Make a second briolette unit.

3 Open a loop (Basics) of a pearl unit. Attach a loop of another pearl unit and close the loop. Attach one more pearl unit. Attach a briolette unit to one loop and complete the wraps.

4 Cut a 1–1¼-in. (2.5–3.2cm) piece of chain. Attach the remaining briolette unit and complete the wraps. Open a 6–7mm jump ring (Basics). Attach the chain dangle and the pearl-and-briolette dangle. Close the jump ring.

5 Attach six to eight pearl units to make a pearl strand approximately 3 in. (7.6cm) long.

6 Decide how long you want your necklace to be. (The blue necklace is 15¼ in./38.7cm; the white, 16 in./41cm.) Divide that number in half and cut three pieces of chain to that length. For the fourth piece, subtract the length of the pearl strand and cut a piece of chain to that length. Attach this piece to the pearl strand's end loop.

7 Open the dangle's jump ring. Attach three chains and the end loop of the pearl-and-chain strand. Close the jump ring.

8 Check the fit, and trim chain if necessary. On one end, use a 4mm jump ring to attach a lobster claw clasp. Repeat on the other end, substituting a soldered jump ring for the clasp.

1 earrings • On a head pin, string a pearl. Make a plain loop (Basics).

2 Cut two 1¼–2-in. (3.2–5cm) pieces of chain. Open the loop of the bead unit (Basics) and attach one end of each chain. Close the loop.

3 Open the loop of an earring wire (Basics). Attach both chains and close the loop. Make a second earring to match the first.

Pearls
interrupted

Searching through cast-off jewelry yields unexpected results

by Cathy Jakicic

This set began as part of a four-pound lot of bulk jewelry — Goodwill Industries auctions jewelry by the pound at shopgoodwill.com — and became a classically styled, understated pearl necklace and earrings. Buying from organizations like Goodwill is a great way to help those who could use a hand, but inexpensive jewelry components can be found in local thrift and resale shops or in the back of Grandma's closet, too.

Tip

Arrange the pearl units on a beading board to get a general idea of the order and spacing before you cut the chain.

Design alternative

Attach a brooch to the chain for a removable pendant.

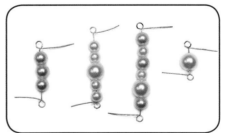

1 necklace • Cut a 3-in. (7.6cm) piece of wire. Make the first half of a wrapped loop (Basics, p. 5) on one end. String three pearls and make the first half of a wrapped loop above the pearl. Repeat, varying the size, number, and color of the pearls in each unit. The total length of the pearl units should be approximately half the length of the chain necklace.

2 a Cut a chain necklace 2–3 in. (5–7.6cm) from one of the ends. **b** If you plan to make earrings, cut a 2-in. (5cm) piece from the remaining chain and set it aside.

3 Attach each chain to a loop of a pearl unit. Complete the wraps.

Updated necklace
and earrings

Supplies

necklace 46 in. (1.2m)
- **50–60** 4–10mm pearls in various colors
- 42–60 in. (1.1–1.5m) 26-gauge half-hard wire
- 2–3-ft. (61–91cm) chain necklace, 3–4mm links
- **2** 5–7mm jump rings (optional)
- lobster claw clasp and soldered jump ring (optional)
- chainnose pliers
- diagonal wire cutters
- roundnose pliers

earrings
- **4** pearls in two sizes
- **2** 11º seed beads
- 2 in. (5cm) chain, cut from necklace
- **2** 2-in. (5cm) head pins
- pair of earring wires
- chainnose pliers
- diagonal wire cutters
- roundnose pliers

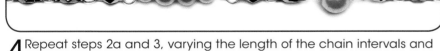

4 Repeat steps 2a and 3, varying the length of the chain intervals and the pearl units until the strand is within 2 in. (5cm) of the desired length. End with a chain.

5 Check the fit. Add or remove pearl units or chain, if desired. If the clasp on the chain is brittle, replace it with a new clasp. First, remove the old clasp and jump ring. Open a new jump ring (Basics). On one end, attach a lobster claw clasp and the chain. Close the jump ring. Repeat on the other end, substituting a soldered jump ring for the clasp.

1 earrings • Cut a ¾-in. (1.9cm) piece of chain. Open the loop of an earring wire and attach the chain. Close the loop.

2 On a head pin, string an 11º seed bead, a large pearl, and a small pearl. Make the first half of a wrapped loop (Basics) above the pearl.

3 Attach the pearl unit to the chain. Complete the wraps. Make a second earring to match the first.

Pearls'

night out

Dress up with a pearl choker and earrings

by Roxie Moede

For a choker that's ready to hit the town, start with a favorite button and add pearls. Or, start with pearls and then hunt for the perfect centerpiece. If you prefer the second option, try your local craft or sewing store for a broad button selection. Then, string this easy, symmetrical jewelry set to make a striking impression.

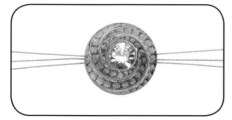

1 necklace • Cut three pieces of beading wire (Basics, p. 5). Over all three wires, center a button.

2 On each end of each wire, string 12 pearls and the corresponding hole of a three-strand spacer bar. Repeat twice. If necessary, string additional pearls until the necklace is within 1 in. (2.5cm) of the length.

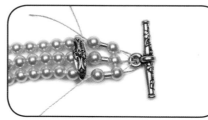

3 On each end of each wire, string a pearl, a crimp bead, and a pearl. On each side, over all three wires, string half of a clasp. Check the fit, and add or remove beads from each end if necessary. Go back through the last few beads strung and tighten the wires. Crimp the crimp beads (Basics) and trim the excess wire.

1 earrings • On a head pin, string: pearl, spacer, pearl, spacer, pearl. Make a plain loop (Basics).

2 Open the loop of an earring wire (Basics). Attach the dangle and close the loop. Make a second earring to match the first.

Design alternative

To make a cuff bracelet with 5 or 6mm pearls, string five strands as a variation on the triple-strand choker.

Supplies

necklace 13½ in. (34.3cm)
- 18–23mm button with shank
- **3** 16-in. (41cm) strands 4mm round pearls
- **6** 14–16mm three-strand spacer bars
- flexible beading wire, .014 or .015
- **6** crimp beads
- toggle clasp
- chainnose or crimping pliers
- diagonal wire cutters

earrings
- **6** 4mm round pearls
- **4** 4–5mm flat spacers
- **2** 1½-in. (3.8cm) head pins
- pair of earring wires
- chainnose pliers
- diagonal wire cutters
- roundnose pliers

Tip

For a choker that lies just right, use Swarovski crystal pearls. Because they're manufactured, the pearls are a uniform size.

Wire

for Special Occasions

Sculpt
a leaf necklace & earrings

Shape and assemble lengths of wire to create this necklace and earrings

by Cynthia Wuller

Complement your wirework by making your own simple hook-and-eye clasp. Flaunt your wireworking skills even more with a pair of earrings suspended from handmade earring wires.

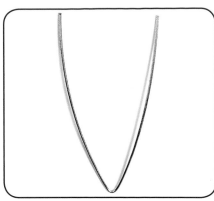

1 necklace • Determine the finished length of your necklace. Cut 18–24 4-in. (10cm) pieces of wire for the large leaves. Cut six 3½-in. (8.9cm) pieces for the medium leaves. Cut six 3-in. (7.6cm) pieces for the small leaves. Bend each wire in half.

Supplies

both projects
◆ chainnose pliers
◆ diagonal wire cutters
◆ mandrel or other cylindrical object
◆ roundnose pliers

silver necklace 15½ in. (39.4cm)
gold necklace 16½ in. (41.9cm)
◆ 16-in. (41cm) strand 4–5mm beads
◆ 14–17 ft. (4.3–5.2m) 20-gauge half-hard wire
◆ bench block or anvil
◆ hammer

earrings
◆ **2** 4–5mm beads
◆ 16 in. (41cm) 20-gauge half-hard wire

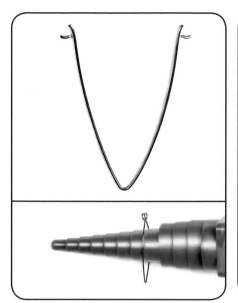

2a To make the leaves: Make a loop at each end of one wire.
b Form the wire around a cylindrical object.

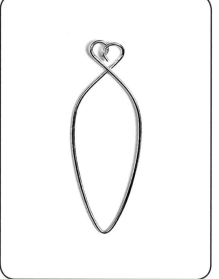

3 Overlap the wire loops as you pull them together. Repeat steps 2 and 3 with the remaining wires.

Tip

The Right Angle mandrel (pictured in step 2) is a useful tool for shaping wire. Visit Fiskars, fiskarscrafts.com, for more information.

4 To make the links: Cut 30–35 1¾-in. (4.4cm) pieces of wire. Make a plain loop (Basics, p. 5) on one end. String a bead and make a plain loop.

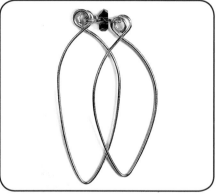

5 To attach the links: Open one loop of a link (Basics). Attach the loops of a large leaf. Close the loop. Repeat with the link's remaining loop and a second large leaf. On each end, use links to attach the remaining large leaves. Attach the medium leaves and then the small leaves.

6 To make a hook-and-eye clasp: Cut a 2½-in. (6.4cm) piece of wire. Make a plain loop on one end. Approximately ½ in. (1.3cm) from the loop, pull the wire around the largest part of your roundnose pliers.

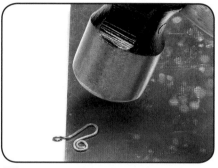

7 Form a coil on the end of the wire, and hammer the hook on a bench block or anvil.

8 Cut a 2½-in. (6.4cm) piece of wire. Make a plain loop on one end. On the other end, make a wrapped loop (Basics) large enough to accommodate the hook.

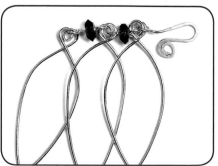

9 On each end, attach half of the clasp to the loops of a leaf.

1 earrings • Cut a 3-in. (7.6cm) piece of wire. Bend the wire in half. Follow steps 2 and 3 of the necklace to make a small leaf. Cut a 1¾-in. (4.4cm) piece of wire. Make a link as in step 4 of the necklace. Open a loop of the link (Basics) and attach the loops of the leaf. Close the loop. Repeat to make a second dangle.

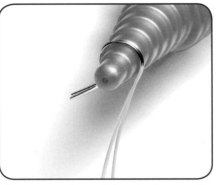

2 Cut two 3-in. (7.6cm) pieces of wire. Make a bend ¼ in. (6mm) from one end of each wire. Pull the wires around a cylindrical object ½ in. (1.3cm) from the bend.

3 Make a single wrapped loop (Basics) on the end of each wire.

4 Open the loop of a dangle and attach an earring wire. Close the loop. Repeat with the second dangle.

Branch
dressing

This necklace looks difficult, but isn't — once you shape the first branch unit, it won't take long to make and connect the remaining ones. Proportional hoop earrings are simple accents that keep the focus rooted in the necklace.

by Jill Italiano

Craft a delicate collar of branches flecked with tiny gemstones

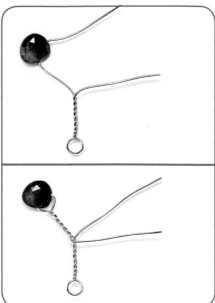

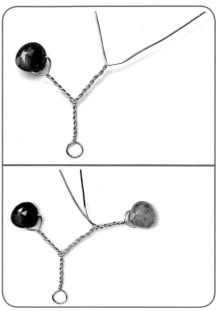

1 **necklace** • Cut a 12-in. (30cm) piece of wire. Using roundnose pliers, make a loop in the center of the wire. Twist the wires together, making a ³⁄₈-in. (1cm) stem.

2a Separate the wires. On one wire, string a top-drilled bead ½ in. (1.3cm) from the end of the stem.

b Twist the wires together to form a branch, stopping when you reach the stem.

3a Twist the wires together to form a ³⁄₈-in. (1cm) branch.

b On the longer wire, string a bead ½ in. (1.3cm) from the branch just made. Bring the longer wire around the bead and twist the wires together to form a branch.

4 Twist the wires together to form a ½-in. (1.3cm) branch. On the longer wire, string a bead ³⁄₈ in. (1cm) from the branch just made. Form a branch.

5 Twist the wires together to form a ³⁄₈-in. (1cm) branch. Make the first half of a wrapped loop (Basics, p. 5). Turn the stem loop perpendicular to the branches. Using roundnose pliers, curve the branches. Make 10 to 12 units.

6 Attach one unit's first half of a wrapped loop to the stem loop of another unit. Complete the wraps. Attach units, flipping every other unit, until the necklace is within 1 in. (2.5cm) of the desired length. Complete the wraps on the end loops.

7 Cut a 2-in. (5cm) piece of wire and center a bead on it. Twist the wires together to make a ¼-in. (6mm) stem above the bead. Make the first half of a wrapped loop above the stem. Cut a 2-in. (5cm) piece of chain for an extender. Attach the loop to the end link of chain and complete the wraps.

8 Open a jump ring (Basics). On one end, attach the end unit's loop and a lobster claw clasp. Close the jump ring. Repeat on the other end, substituting the chain extender for the clasp.

Tip

In steps 2 and 3 of the necklace, remember to string the second and third beads of each unit on the longer wire. This will ensure that enough wire remains for the wrapped loop.

Supplies

10-unit necklace 15 in. (38cm)
- **31–37** 4–5mm beads, top drilled
- 10½–12½ ft. (3.2–3.8m) 26-gauge dead-soft wire
- 2 in. (5cm) chain for extender, 4–5mm links
- **2** 3–4mm jump rings
- lobster claw clasp
- chainnose pliers
- diagonal wire cutters
- roundnose pliers

earrings
- **2** 4–5mm beads, top drilled
- 7 in. (18cm) 20-gauge half-hard wire
- 5 in. (13cm) 26-gauge dead-soft wire
- chainnose pliers
- ballpeen hammer
- bench block or anvil
- diagonal wire cutters
- metal file or emery board
- roundnose pliers

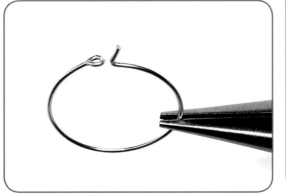

1 **earrings** • Cut a 2½-in. (6.4cm) piece of 26-gauge wire. String a top-drilled bead and make a set of wraps above it (Basics). Make a wrapped loop (Basics) above the wraps.

2 Cut a 3½-in. (8.9cm) piece of 20-gauge wire. Wrap the wire around a 15–20mm-diameter pen barrel or other round object. Make a plain loop (Basics) on one end of the wire. Bend the other end up to form a right angle. Trim the excess wire to ⅛ in. (3mm) and file the end.

3 Hammer the hoop on a bench block or anvil, avoiding the loop and bent end. Turn the hoop over and hammer the other side. String the bead unit. Make a second earring to match the first.

.Tiers of joy

Teardrop components frame simple earrings

by Karey Grant

Supplies

- ◆ **4** 42mm teardrop components (The Bead Shop, beadshop.com)
- ◆ **2** 10–14mm briolettes
- ◆ **2** 3–4mm spacers
- ◆ 20 in. (51cm) 24-gauge half-hard wire
- ◆ pair of earring wires
- ◆ chainnose pliers
- ◆ diagonal wire cutters
- ◆ roundnose pliers

Big-impact earrings can be tricky: Often earrings that are heavy in impact also weigh down your lobes! For earrings that are large yet lightweight, try delicate teardrop lines. The clean, simple style is always elegant and offers an opportunity to frame a favorite gemstone.

1 Cut a 7-in. (18cm) piece of wire. String a briolette and cross the ends above it, leaving a ³⁄₈-in. (1cm) stem. With the stem, make a plain loop (Basics, p. 5) perpendicular to the briolette.

2 Grasping the plain loop with chainnose pliers, use your fingers to wrap the wire around the top of the briolette. Trim the excess wire. Use chainnose pliers to tuck the end under the wraps. Open the plain loop (Basics) and attach the inner loop of a teardrop component. Close the loop.

3 Cut a 3-in. (7.6cm) piece of wire. Make the first half of a wrapped loop on one end. String a spacer and make the first half of a wrapped loop (Basics).

4 Attach one loop of the spacer unit and the outer loop of the teardrop-and-briolette component. Attach the remaining loop of the spacer unit and the inner loop of another teardrop component. Complete the wraps.

5 Open the loop of an earring wire (Basics) and attach the dangle. Close the loop. Make a second earring to match the first.

Tip

• If you use smaller briolettes, wrap them with 26-gauge wire. In step 1, make the first half of a wrapped loop instead of a plain loop. Attach the teardrop component in step 2 and wrap both wires when you complete the wraps.
• For added texture, gently hammer the wire components.

Maid to order

Customize earrings for a wedding party

by Jane Konkel

In a wedding party, the bride and each bridesmaid have their own aesthetic, so why not design jewelry to reflect each woman's individual style? These handmade designs will get you on your way to the Big Day.

Tip

For a bridesmaid without pierced ears, try these designs with a pair of clip-on style earring wires.

modern maid

1 modern maid · Cut a 6-in. (15cm) piece of wire. String: briolette, 3mm bicone crystal, briolette, 3mm, briolette. Center the beads on the wire. String both ends through a 4mm bicone in opposite directions.

2 Bend each end of the wire upward. On each end, string a 3mm and a 4mm. On a bench block or anvil, hammer each side of a link.

3 Wrap each wire end tightly around the link four times. With chainnose pliers, press each end to the back of the link.

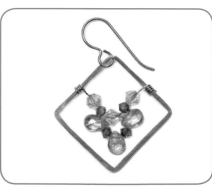

4 Open the loop of an earring wire (Basics, p. 5) and attach the link. Close the loop. Make a second earring to match the first.

1 *classic bride* • Cut a 5-in. (13cm) piece of wire. Alternate four bicone crystals with three briolettes. Center the beads on the wire.

2 Place the center briolette at the base of a link and bend each end of the wire upward. Wrap each end tightly around the link five times. With chainnose pliers, press each end to the back of the link.

3 On a bench block or anvil, hammer each side of two jump rings. Open one jump ring (Basics) and attach the link. Close the jump ring. Use the second jump ring to attach the dangle and a loop of an earring wire. Make a second earring to match the first.

classic bride

Supplies

classic bride
- **6** 5–7mm cubic zirconia briolettes
- **8** 3mm bicone crystals
- **2** 28mm marquise links (The Earth Bazaar, theearthbazaar.com)
- 10 in. (25cm) 26-gauge half-hard wire
- **4** 6mm jump rings
- pair of earring wires with CZs
- chainnose and roundnose pliers, or **2** pairs of chainnose pliers
- diagonal wire cutters
- bench block or anvil
- hammer

modern maid
- **6** 5–7mm cubic zirconia briolettes
- **6** 4mm bicone crystals
- **8** 3mm bicone crystals
- **2** 21mm square links (Rings & Things, rings-things.com,)
- 12 in. (30cm) 26-gauge half-hard wire
- pair of earring wires
- chainnose and roundnose pliers, or **2** pairs of chainnose pliers
- diagonal wire cutters
- bench block or anvil
- hammer

gypsy maid
- **8** 5–7mm cubic zirconia briolettes
- **2** 37mm marquise links (Rings & Things)
- 64 in. (1.6m) 26-gauge half-hard wire
- **8** 3–4 mm jump rings
- pair of earring wires
- bench block or anvil
- chainnose pliers
- diagonal wire cutters
- hammer
- roundnose pliers

1 gypsy maid • Cut an 8-in. (20cm) piece of wire. String a briolette and make a set of wraps above it (Basics). Make the first half of a wrapped loop (Basics) above the wraps. Make four briolette units.

2 Grasp the loop with chainnose pliers. Using your fingers, wrap the wire around the top of the briolette.

3 On a bench block or anvil, hammer each side of a link. Open a jump ring (Basics) and attach a briolette unit and the link. Close the jump ring. Use jump rings to attach two more briolette units.

4 Open the loop of an earring wire (Basics). Attach the dangle and close the loop. Use a jump ring to attach the remaining briolette unit and the loop of the earring wire. Make a second earring to match the first.

gypsy maid

Suspended
briolette

Dangle a drop of color in the center of a gracefully arching wire pendant

by Tamira Williams

Beautiful briolettes are often sold singly, making this project the perfect place to showcase one. Use silver wire to match the cool colors of the season, or warm up with glowing gold. But have no fear for the safety of your stone — tiny wraps keep it suspended without the suspense.

Supplies

necklace 22 in. (56cm)

- 16–23mm gemstone briolette
- **2** 6mm bicone crystals
- 7½ in. (19.1cm) 16-gauge half-hard wire
- 14 in. (36cm) 22-gauge half-hard wire
- 16–20 in. (41–50cm) chain, 2–4mm links
- **2** 4–5mm jump rings
- lobster claw clasp and soldered jump ring
- chainnose pliers
- diagonal wire cutters
- Right Angle mandrel (Fiskars, fiskarscrafts.com)
- roundnose pliers

1 Cut a 1½-in. (3.8cm) piece of 22-gauge wire and make a plain loop (Basics, p. 5) on one end. String a bicone crystal and make a plain loop. Make a second bicone unit. Set aside for step 6.

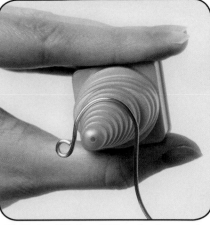

2 Cut a 7½-in. (19.1cm) piece of 16-gauge wire. Make a loop on each end. With the loops facing up, wrap one end of the wire halfway around a mandrel or small round object. Repeat on the other end of the wire.

3 Center the mandrel and pull the ends of the wire together to form an open teardrop shape.

4 Cut a 4-in. (10cm) piece of 22-gauge wire and center a briolette. Wrap one end of the wire around one side of the teardrop, just below the opening. Make four wraps. Trim the wire and tuck the end. Repeat on the other side.

5 Cut a 7-in. (15cm) piece of 22-gauge wire. Wrap the wire around the teardrop six to nine times to close it.

Wrap once around one side of the teardrop, then around the other side in the opposite direction. Make five or six figure-8 wraps. Trim the wire and tuck the end.

6 Cut two 8–10-in. (20–25cm) pieces of chain. On each side, open the loops (Basics) of a bicone unit. Attach one loop to one side of the pendant and the other loop to a chain. Close the loops.

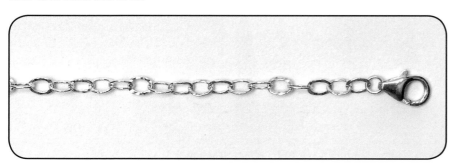

7 Open a jump ring (Basics) and attach an end link of chain and a lobster claw clasp. Repeat on the other end, substituting a soldered jump ring for the clasp.

Design alternative

Loop the ends of the 16-gauge wire in opposite directions before pulling the ends together. Hammer the wire for texture and string a chain through one loop.

Briolettes
unwrapped

A simple design turns top-drilled beads into earrings

by Jill Alexander

If you love briolettes, but don't enjoy making wrapped loops, here's an easy solution: Showcase each bead on a curved, coiled head pin. Experiment with your beads and head pins, or add crystal dangles for extra sparkle.

Supplies

- **2** 10–15mm briolettes
- **2** 2½-in. (6.4cm) 22-gauge decorative head pins
- pair of earring wires
- bench block or anvil
- chainnose pliers
- Fiskars Right Angle mandrel (fiskarscrafts.com)
- hammer
- roundnose pliers

1 Wrap the decorative end of a head pin around a mandrel or the barrel of a pen.

2 String a briolette. With your roundnose pliers, make a loop at the end of the head pin. Make a coil (see tip below).

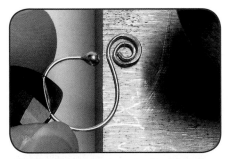

3 Gently hammer each side of the coil.

4 Open the loop of an earring wire (Basics, p. 5). Attach the dangle and close the loop. Make a second earring in the mirror image of the first.

Tip

Use chainnose pliers to grasp the coil as you continue spiraling the wire with your fingers.

Design alternative

If you use center-drilled beads in these earrings, string a bead and then curve the head pin around it, rather than curving the head pin first.

From Trendy to Traditional

The *Easy Beading* Series Has It All!

Jewelry is a hallmark of personal style and this outstanding collection from *BeadStyle* magazine has something for every preference. The *Easy Beading* series is a prized collectible for loyal readers as well as a rich resource for those new to beading. Beginning beaders can get up to speed in no time with the clear, illustrated Beader's Glossary and Basics sections. Every project has been tested by *BeadStyle* editors, so beaders can get started with confidence! The instructions are clear and the end results are terrific, whether to wear or share as gifts.

Easy Beading Vol. 6
Fast. Fashionable. Fun.

From the publisher of
BeadStyle magazine

62915 • $29.95

62172 • $29.95

62261 • $29.95

62410 • $29.95

62632 • $29.95

62885 • $29.95

Buy now from your favorite bead or craft shop!

**Or at www.KalmbachStore.com
or 1-800-533-6644**

Monday – Friday, 8:30 a.m. – 4:30 p.m. CST.
Outside the United States and Canada
call 262-796-8776, ext. 661.

KB KALMBACH BOOKS

Contributors

Jill Alexander likes to leave her beads on a design board so she can look at them throughout the day. She's always thinking about her projects, even when she's busy doing other things. Contact Jill at jnj7493@sbcglobal.net.

Lori Anderson is a full-time jewelry designer living in Easton, Md. When she designs at her kitchen table, she opts to watch *CSI*-type shows instead of listening to background music. Contact her at lori@lorianderson. net or visit lorianderson.net.

Patrica Bartlein is co-owner of Northwest Beads in Menomonee Falls, Wis. She enjoys inspiring customers of all ages to bead. Contact her at Northwest Beads at 262-255-4740, via e-mail at northwestbeaders@sbcglobal.net, or visit northwestbeads.com.

Arleen Bejerano is a jewelry designer in Lincoln, Neb. Contact her via e-mail at arbejerano@hotmail.com.

Jackie Boettcher, who is a credit assistant for Kalmbach Publishing Co., is often inspired by her wardrobe when it comes to creating jewelry. If she has an outfit with no jewelry to match, she challenges herself to make something that goes with that outfit and some of her other clothes, too. Contact her at jboettcher@kalmbach.com.

Karin Buckingham is the author of *Altered You!, Mostly Metals: A Beginners Guide to Jewelry Design*, and *The Absolute Beginner's Guide: Stringing Beaded Jewelry*. A longtime jewelry designer and former associate editor for *BeadStyle* magazine, Karin now works as an associate editor for Kalmbach Books. Visit her blog, artfulcrafts. blogspot.com.

Angie D'Amato's most important tip for beginning jewelry makers is to explore different jewelry-making styles and techniques. She believes that because there are so many ways to make jewelry, and so many materials, eventually you'll find a technique to reflect your style and personality. Contact Angie in care of Kalmbach Books.

Naomi Fujimoto wonders if she inherited her love of jewelry from her grandfather: When he traveled, he often brought back jewelry. Naomi is Senior Editor of *BeadStyle* magazine and the author of *Cool Jewels: Beading Projects for Teens*. Visit her blog at cooljewelsnaomi.blogspot. com, or contact her via e-mail at nfujimoto@beadstyle.com.

Mia Gofar is the author of several how-to jewelry books published in Indonesia. Her first book was released in 2005, and she continues to write books today. Contact Mia via e-mail at mia@miagofar.com, or visit her website, miagofar.com or miamoredesign.com.

Karey Grant's beading advice: "Stop thinking and start doing. An instructor of mine told me, 'You aren't an artist if you are thinking about art. You are an artist if you are creating art.'" Contact Karey via her website, inspiredbystones.com.

Linda Arline Hartung is co-owner of Alacarte Clasps™ and WireLace®, and a designer/ teacher and Ambassador for CREATE-YOUR-STYLE with CRYSTALLIZED™ - *Swarovski Elements*. Her designs and techniques have been featured in beading and jewelry-making publications around the world. Contact her via e-mail at linda@ alacarteclasps.com, or visit her websites, alacarteclasps.com or wirelace.com.

Jill Italiano is a full-time jewelry designer and manufacturer.

Contact her via e-mail at jill.i@jillidesigns.com, or visit her website, jillidesigns.com.

Cathy Jakicic is Editor of *BeadStyle* magazine and the author of the book *Hip Handmade Memory Jewelry*. She has been creating jewelry for more than 15 years. Contact her via e-mail at cjakicic@beadstyle.com.

Jane Konkel is Associate Editor of *BeadStyle*, and contributed many of her own new designs to the book *Bead Journey*. Contact her via e-mail at jkonkel@ beadstyle.com.

Irina Miech is an artist, teacher, and the author of *Beautiful Wire Jewelry for Beaders* and *Beautiful Wire Jewelry for Beaders 2*, as well as a growing series of books on metal clay for beaders. She also oversees her retail bead supply business and classroom studio, Eclectica and The Bead Studio in Brookfield, Wis., where she teaches classes in beading, wirework, and metal clay. Contact Irina at Eclectica, 262-641-0910, or via e-mail at eclecticainfo@sbcglobal.net.

Formerly Editorial Associate of *BeadStyle*, **Lindsay Mikulsky** is currently pursuing a career in education. Contact her at lindsayrose5@gmail.com.

Roxie Moede works in the credit department at Kalmbach Publishing Co. Her favorite place to bead? In the rec room downstairs with her cat sleeping next to her. Contact Roxie at roxie@wi.rr.com.

Kathie Scrimgeour has been a jewelry designer since 2004. Contact her via e-mail at kjscrim@yahoo.com.

Sara Strauss was trained in jewelry design at the Fashion Institute of Technology in New York. Contact her via e-mail at

bluestaro@hotmail.com, or visit her websites, sgsjewelry.com and sgsjewelry.etsy.com.

Jewelry designer **Kellie Sutton** recently opened her own bead store, Kellie's Bead Boutique, in Maple Ridge, British Columbia, Canada. Contact her via e-mail at kellie@kelliesbeadboutique. com, or visit her website, kelliesbeadboutique.com.

Debbie Tuttle is a full-time jewelry artist who creates her own vintage-inspired jewelry in Charlton, N.Y. Contact her via e-mail at bijouxcreations@ hotmail.com, or visit her website, bijouxcreations.com.

Jenny Van is a microbiologist and jewelry designer based in Huntington Beach, Calif. Contact her via e-mail at jenny@beadsj.com, or visit her website, beadsj.com.

Tamira Williams has been creating bohemian-influenced jewelry since 2003. Contact her via e-mail at raiynecharms@msn. com, or visit raiynecharms.com.

Cynthia B. Wuller, the author of *Inspired Wire*, holds a Bachelor of Fine Arts degree from the School of the Art Institute of Chicago. She has contributed to *Art Jewelry* and *BeadStyle* magazines, and her work can be found in a number of books such as *Easy Beading Vol. 4, The Art of Jewelry: Paper Jewelry, The Art of Jewelry: Wood*, and *Beading with Pearls*. She lives in Chicago with her husband. Contact Cynthia at cbwuller@yahoo.com.